![Sesame Street 123]

All about FIREFIGHTERS

Jennifer Boothroyd

Lerner Publications ◆ Minneapolis

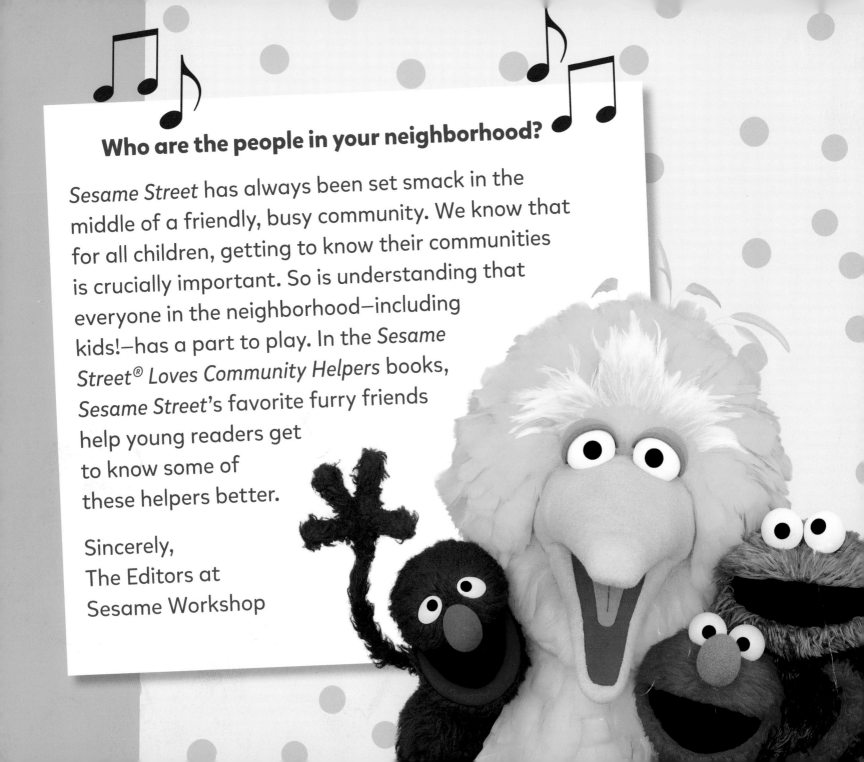

Who are the people in your neighborhood?

Sesame Street has always been set smack in the middle of a friendly, busy community. We know that for all children, getting to know their communities is crucially important. So is understanding that everyone in the neighborhood—including kids!—has a part to play. In the *Sesame Street® Loves Community Helpers* books, *Sesame Street*'s favorite furry friends help young readers get to know some of these helpers better.

Sincerely,
The Editors at
Sesame Workshop

Table of Contents

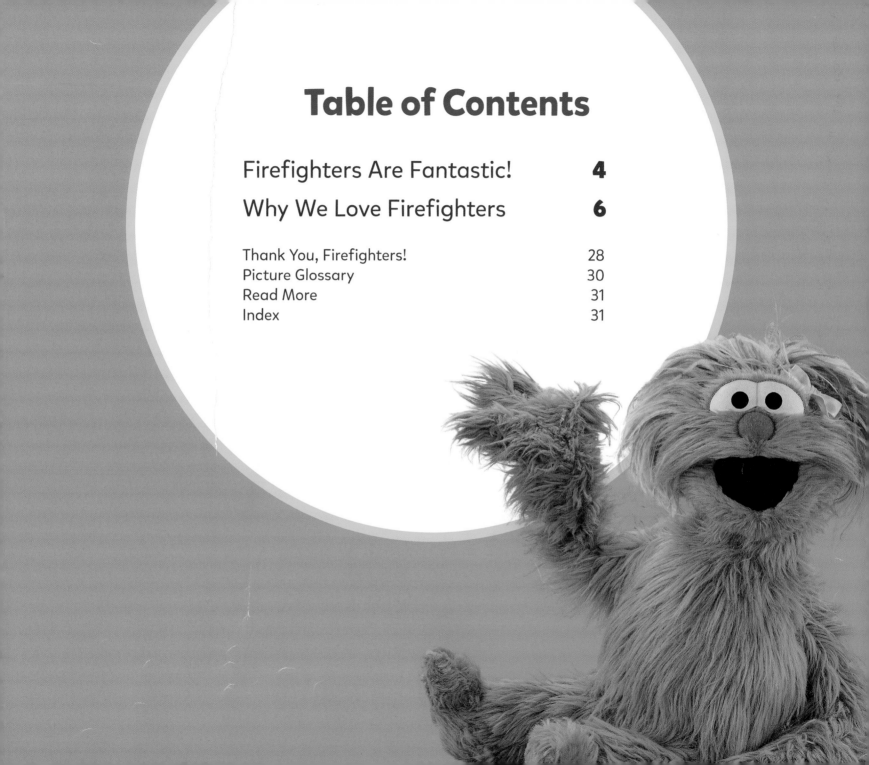

Firefighters Are Fantastic!

Firefighters keep people safe. They are heroes just like adorable little me, Super Grover.

Why We Love Firefighters

Firefighters are community helpers.

Firefighters are there when people need help.

They put out fires. They help when someone is hurt.

7

Firefighters work at fire stations.

They keep their tools and fire trucks at the station.

Firefighters visit schools. They show people how to be safe.

Firefighters practice getting ready. They are quick during an emergency.

Practice makes perfect!

13

Firefighters wear special clothes that protect them.

They wear helmets, boots, pants, jackets, and gloves.

15

Too much smoke from a fire can make you sick. Face masks help firefighters breathe clean air.

17

Firefighters have flashlights to see in the dark.

They use radios to talk to one another.

Fire trucks get firefighters to fires quickly. Fire trucks have sirens and flashing lights.

Fire trucks have ladders and hoses.

Ladders help firefighters climb really high!

Firefighters use hoses to put out a fire.

Firefighters need to be strong. They carry lots of tools. They climb stairs and ladders quickly.

Running keeps me strong and healthy.

Firefighters are brave. Firefighters work together to keep everyone safe!

Heroes get scared too. But they have the courage—and the training—to keep going!

Thank You, Firefighters!

Be a hero! Write a thank-you letter to the firefighters in your community.

Dear Firefighters,

I know being a hero is hard work! Thank you for helping everyone in our community. I feel safe knowing you are here.

Your friend,

Super Grover

Picture Glossary

breathe: take air into your body through your nose or mouth

community: a place where people live and work

courage: the ability to do what is scary or hard

emergency: when something dangerous or very serious happens

Read More

Bellisario, Gina. *Firefighters in My Community.* Minneapolis: Lerner Publications, 2019.

Evans, Shira. *Helpers in your Neighborhood.* Washington, DC: National Geographic Kids, 2018.

Waxman, Laura Hamilton. *Firefighter Tools.* Minneapolis: Lerner Publications, 2020.

Index

Photo Acknowledgments

Additional image credits: kali9/Getty Images, pp. 5, 17, 30; Blend Images-PBNJ Productions/Getty Images, p. 6; Westend61/Getty Images, p. 7; AlenaPaulus/Getty Images, pp. 8, 13; Hero Images/Getty Images, pp. 9–10, 27, 30; Axel Bueckert/EyeEm/Getty Images, p. 11; Corbis/VCG/Getty Images, pp. 12, 29–30; LPETTET/Getty Images, pp. 14, 16, 30; Kris Timken/Getty Images, p. 15; FXQuadro/Getty Images, p. 18; LightField Studios/Shutterstock.com, p. 19; LeoPatrizi/Getty Images, p. 20; Firefighter Montreal/Shutterstock.com, p. 22; freedomnaruk/Shutterstock.com, p. 23; Radius Images/Getty Images, p. 24; monkeybusinessimages/Getty Images, p. 26; Sergey Mironov/Shutterstock.com, p.25.

Cover: Hero Images/Getty Images.

Lerner Publications Company
An imprint of Lerner Publishing Group, Inc.
241 First Avenue North
Minneapolis, MN 55401 USA

For reading levels and more information, look up this title at www.lernerbooks.com.

Main body text set in Mikado Medium.
Typeface provided by HVD Fonts.

Editor: Rebecca Higgins **Designer:** Emily Harris **Photo Editor:** Rebecca Higgins
Lerner team: Martha Kranes and Katy Prozinski

Library of Congress Cataloging-in-Publication Data

Names: Boothroyd, Jennifer, 1972- author.
Title: All about firefighters / Jennifer Boothroyd.
Description: Minneapolis, MN : Lerner Publications, [2020] | Series: Sesame Street ® loves community helpers | Includes bibliographical references and index. | Audience: Ages 4-8 | Audience: Grades K-1 | Summary: "Every community needs firefighters! Firefighters keep people safe by putting out fires and teaching fire safety. Join Grover and friends in this fun approach to key curricular content and learn all about firefighters"— Provided by publisher.
Identifiers: LCCN 2019039933 (print) | LCCN 2019039934 (ebook) | ISBN 9781541589957 (library binding) | ISBN 9781728400938 (ebook)
Subjects: LCSH: Firefighters—Juvenile literature. | Fire extinction—Juvenile literature.
Classification: LCC HD8039.F5 B66 2020 (print) | LCC HD8039.F5 (ebook) | DDC 363.73—dc23

LC record available at https://lccn.loc.gov/2019039933
LC ebook record available at https://lccn.loc.gov/2019039934

Manufactured in the United States of America
1-47505-48049-11/20/2019